driven to win:
A.J. FOYT

Author

Mike Kupper

Photography

**Heinz Kluetmeier
Lewis Franck
Richard Weening
Vernon J. Biever
Joe DiMaggio**

RAINTREE EDITIONS

2489

Copyright © 1975 by Advanced Learning Concepts, Inc.
International copyrights reserved in all countries.
No part of this book may be reproduced in any form
without written permission of the publisher.
Library of Congress Number: 75-19276

Published by **Raintree Editions**
A Division of Raintree Publishers Ltd.
Milwaukee, Wisconsin 53203

Distributed by Childrens Press
1224 West Van Buren Street
Chicago, Illinois 60607

Library of Congress Cataloging in Publication Data

Kupper, Mike.
    Driven to win, A. J. Foyt.

    SUMMARY: A brief biography of the race car driver who has won the United States Auto Club Championship five times and the Indy 500 three times.
    1. Foyt, A. J., 1935-   —Juvenile literature.
2. Automobile racing—Juvenile literature. [1. Foyt, A. J., 1935-   2. Automobile racing—Biography]
I. Kluetmeier, Heinz. II. Title.
GV1032.F66K86   796.7′2′0924 [B] [92]   75-19276
ISBN 0-8172-0121-1
ISBN 0-8172-0120-3 lib. bdg.

Contents

1 One Tough Texan   4
2 Fancypants   12
3 Feudin', Fussin', and Fightin'   18
4 Peaks and Valleys   26
5 The Checkered Flag   35
6 The Financial Foyt   43

One Tough Texan

The A. J. in A. J. Foyt does not stand for Always Jolly.

A jolly man would not threaten to beat up an elderly race promoter.

He would not storm into another driver's pit, seeking revenge for an incident on the track.

He would not throw a handful of steel sockets from a ratchet wrench at his mechanic.

He would not fire a mechanic for taking a supper break.

He would not come down so often or so hard on the organization in which he does most of his racing.

And, he probably would not be generally recognized as the best, toughest, most versatile race driver in the United States, maybe the world. Not if that jolly man still went by the name of A. J. Foyt. He might be a winner, but he wouldn't be Foyt.

Foyt, in his long and brilliant career, has done all of those things. He also has won more races, more money, more glory, and more fans than any other all-around driver ever has, or probably ever will.

Age may have mellowed Foyt slightly, but only slightly. He is not quite so quick to anger now, but still quicker than most. He still demands that his cars be prepared just so.

And he still drives to win. For winning is what Foyt is all about. He drives to win because he is driven to win. There may be very many other important things in the world, but very few of them are as important to him as winning a race.

"Winning is first," he says. Forget the idea of competing for the fun of competition.

"I run all the races the same. I run to win. I don't care if I win $100,000 or $1,000, I just want to win. There's no other thrill like it. If you don't want to win, why race? You know, I honestly do think I'm going to win every race I'm in. And when I do, I'm happy. When I don't, I go down like it's my first race.

"I like to be a winner. If you leave a racetrack a winner, people always remember you. If you lead every lap but that last one, the next day somebody asks, 'Who finished second?' and nobody remembers. They only remember who won."

Such statements would lead one to believe that the tough Texan from Houston is a straightforward sort of guy who believes what he says, and says what he believes. And he is. Sometimes.

But Foyt is living proof that almost nothing in this world is quite as simple as it seems. There have been races that he must have known he could not win. But he still drove, and still tried. There have been other races — a few — that he did not try to win. What he said yesterday does not necessarily apply today. Nor will what he says today necessarily apply tomorrow.

Foyt's career is as studded with contradictions and controversies as it is with victories.

He has complained bitterly about cheating by others in racing. Yet many of those in racing, where cheating is a part of the business, consider him the most successful rule bender of all time.

He has criticized the dizzying speeds at which drivers must race. But he has not slowed down himself.

In moments of depression, he has threatened to quit racing. But after more than a quarter century on the track, he still is hard at it, and he still is winning.

Foyt may be many things, but he is not a simple person.

If winning is what he's all about, though, there is no question that he has been a rousing success, in whatever form of racing he has tried.

Foyt is best known for his driving in the United States Auto Club's championship car division, often known simply as Indy car racing. He has been USAC's national champion a record six times. He is one of only four drivers to have won the Indianapolis 500 three times, and the only driver ever to have won each of USAC's 500-mile races—at Indianapolis; Ontario, California; and Mt. Pocono, Pennsylvania.

In 1975, with his career still going strong, he had won more than 50 of USAC's national championship races, a total that puts him far ahead of any other driver, past or present. His closest competitor in USAC, Mario Andretti, had won 32.

He also has been a winner in USAC's other divisions. He was the 1968 champion in the late model stock car division, and over the years has won 29 races in that class. He was USAC's Eastern Zone sprint car champion in 1960, and by 1975 had won 28 races in that division.

USAC separated its championship division from dirt track racing in 1971. A new division was set up for championship cars on dirt. In 1972, Foyt won two of the four dirt track events and the title in that division. He never has been USAC's champion in the midget car division. He quit driving midgets regularly many years ago. But he has won 20 midget feature races.

In late 1974 and early 1975, USAC came up with a World Series of Auto Racing, in which its leading drivers ran four races, one each in championship, stock, sprint, and midget cars. Foyt won it. He was first in the stock and sprint car events. He finished fourth in the Indy car event after his car ran out of fuel while he was leading. He was sixth in the midget race.

Even if Foyt had raced strictly in USAC, all of that would be impressive. But there is more.

Foyt also has been a frequent guest driver in the National Association for Stock Car Auto Racing, and has won often in that circuit as well. In 1972, in fact, he won the Daytona 500, NASCAR's biggest event.

For most of his career, he has been an oval track driver. But now and then he has tried road racing, where instead of always turning left over a flat or banked oval course, drivers must drive uphill and down, turning left and right. His reputation has not suffered in road races. In 1963 he went to Nassau's Speed Week in the Bahamas and won twice in

sports cars. And in 1967 he gained worldwide fame when he and Dan Gurney, his co-driver, won the LeMans 24-hour endurance race in France. That was his first, and last, drive at LeMans.

There is little doubt that Foyt would have matched his USAC success in any other style of racing if he had competed in it regularly. And he has a simple explanation for the victories he has scored on the high-banked southern stock car tracks and twisting road courses.

"Any race driver, if he's any good, can adapt himself," he says. "If he can't adapt, he shouldn't be driving."

Still, Foyt seems able to adapt himself easier than many other drivers. In 1964, for instance, he went to NASCAR's Firecracker 400 at Daytona Beach, intending to drive a Ford. After practicing in the car, he decided that he didn't like it. So he accepted a ride in a Dodge.

He had never driven the Dodge before. He took it out for practice and promptly bounced it off the wall. The car was wrecked and Foyt was shaken up, but the next day — race day — he jumped into another Dodge and drove it to victory.

That sort of nerve and determination has marked Foyt's career from the start. But the big thing in winning, he maintains, is proper preparation. In his garage at the Indianapolis Speedway hangs a sign that says, "Luck is when preparation meets opportunity."

Drivers have to do the best they can with what they have. Foyt always tries to have something a little better than everyone else.

When Foyt does not win, he is a hard man to live with. When he does not win because his equipment failed him, he can be downright dangerous. He yells a lot, too.

But he says there is good reason for yelling. "Sometimes you have to holler to keep everybody sharp. When something goes wrong, I get real disappointed. In racing, you make your own luck. When guys sit around instead of working, you fall down. The way to stay on top is to keep on working. If I have to holler at somebody to keep them working, I'll holler.

"You know why I'm faster? Because I outdrive 'em. And I outsmart 'em. That's why we build our own cars — to have better equipment. If I have to drive 'em, I want to know that everything's done right.

"There's a time for work and a time for fun. We can have fun later. Right now, let's win the race."

No, indeed, the A. J. in A. J. Foyt does not stand for Always Jolly.

Fancypants

Anthony Joseph. That's what the A. J. stands for. Altogether, he's A. J. Foyt, Jr.

Nobody calls him Anthony. Nobody calls him Junior. And almost nobody calls him Tony. A. J. Foyt, Sr., is known as Tony. A. J. is known simply as A. J. That's what he has painted on his driving helmets. But he is also called Tex, Super Tex, The King, and, by some who think it's a fitting name for a race driver, A. J. Foot.

He once had another nickname, too. Very early in his career, he drove midget races in spotless white trousers. White is hardly a practical color to wear at dusty dirt tracks or around greasy race cars and engines. Most drivers wore coveralls, clothes more suited to their sport. They laughingly referred to Foyt as Fancypants.

The white pants might have been a gimmick, something to draw attention to himself and away from some of the better known drivers. Once he began winning, Foyt gave up the white pants and let his driving draw the attention.

There are those who maintain that Foyt was born to squeeze into the cockpit of a race car and try to make it go fast. Whether or not that's true, he certainly was exposed to racing at a young enough age.

Tony Foyt, his father, owned midget cars. A. J. was being taken to races as a baby. When A. J. was three years old, his father gave him a pedal-operated red racer. "I thought that little ol' car was the most beautiful thing there ever was," A. J. says.

By the time A. J. was five, Tony Foyt had built him a scaled-down midget, complete with a three-horsepower engine. The car could go 50 miles an hour. So A. J. drove it that fast in exhibition runs between races at a Houston track.

What Foyt didn't learn at the track, he was picking up at his father's garage, a gathering place for race drivers. He watched, listened, and helped with the mechanical work whenever he could. He also worked on his own little car. And often, when nobody was looking, he took it out on the streets to test it. That was not much appreciated by the neighbors, or the Houston police.

The young Foyt was eager to try the real thing, though. And finally he did, one night in 1946 when he was 11 years old. "I owned two midget cars in those days," his father said. "Mrs. Foyt and I took one of them to Dallas for a race. We left one of them home, and we left A. J. home, too.

"When we got back, we found the whole yard torn up. The grass was chewed to pieces and there were tire gouges all over. The swings we had in the yard had been knocked down. I knew right away that A. J. had got some of his buddies to push him and they had got that midget started up.

"And then, when I went into the garage and saw the midget, I knew why A. J. had quit. He caught the thing on fire and burned up the engine. It was sitting there with the paint all scorched.

"I went into the house and right into his bedroom. He played like he was asleep, but he wasn't. I didn't get him up, but I knew right then, standing there in that kid's room, that he would have to race. There just wasn't going to be any other way. The next day, I told him, 'If you want to race, all

right, race. But promise to always drive something good.'"

By the time he was 17, Foyt had quit high school and was racing full time, before he was of legal racing age. "I couldn't study anymore," he said. "I was racing for my dad and working in his garage and taking home $75 a week and you know how it is. I just couldn't wait any longer."

A. J. was impatient as a driver, too, even as a youngster. In his first legal race, a midget event in Houston, he had one of his temper tantrums.

"He took the car out, drove around a few laps, then came back in mad," his father recalls. "He was cussin' and stompin'. 'Can't we get this hunk of junk to go any faster?' he'd snort. He did that until someone told him he'd just broken the track record."

Foyt continued racing midgets and modified stock cars. At first he raced just around Houston, but he quickly expanded his territory to cover Texas, then the entire Southwest.

He got into sprint cars, too. He began racing in the Midwest and East, where there was more sprint car action.

Sprint car racing was very big in the 1950s, when Foyt was coming up through the ranks. Many still consider it the truest test of an oval track driver. And most real fans still see it as the most dangerous kind of racing.

Sprint cars are nearly as big, nearly as powerful, and nearly as fast as the old-style Indianapolis roadster. But instead of being raced on long, wide, paved tracks, sprint cars are usually raced on oily, slippery, half-mile or quarter-mile dirt tracks. Foyt and sprint cars got along like peanut butter and jelly.

"I always liked sprint car racing because I was good at it," Foyt said. "Sprint cars race on dirt tracks, and I was always good on dirt. Racing dirt, on a short track, it's more the driver than the car, and I like that."

Before the change to the lighter, rear-engine Indy cars in the mid-1960s, the best way to hitch a ride on the championship trail was to win in sprint cars. Owners and chief mechanics watched the sprints for impressive young talent.

Foyt was impressive. He didn't back down, on the track or off. He was establishing two reputations, one as a driver to be respected, the other as a hothead who liked to settle disputes with his fists.

Foyt's rise was swift. By 1957, at 22, he had landed a place in the championship car circuit. He still was driving sprints and midgets, and his championship car was not the fastest. But his potential was there for all to see.

The next year, Foyt jumped to Al Dean's team, one of the better outfits in racing then. But after two years with Dean and mechanic Clint Brawner, and no Indy car victories, Foyt left.

In 1960, he joined car owner Bob Bowes and mechanic George Bignotti, and his career took an immediate turn for the better.

He scored his first championship victory that year on the dirt at DuQuoin, Illinois. He went on to three other victories, all in 100-mile races, and won the national championship.

In 1961, he scored the first of his Indianapolis victories and successfully defended his national title. At 26, he was an Indianapolis 500 winner and a two-time national champion. Some men drive professionally for 26 years and never come close to winning either an Indy 500 or a national championship.

Nobody called Foyt Fancypants anymore. And he really was just getting started.

Feudin', Fussin', and Fightin'

A. J. Foyt doesn't exactly look for trouble. But he doesn't exactly run away from it, either.

As somebody once said of him, "He'd fight a bear with a stick, and give the bear first licks." As far as anyone knows, A. J. never has tangled with a bear. But he has taken on—sometimes with words and sometimes with fists—mechanics, other drivers, sportswriters, promoters, and the entire United States Auto Club.

His battles with mechanic George Bignotti have become legendary. Drivers and mechanics often have their differences. But when Foyt and Bignotti were teammates, they almost never agreed. About the only thing that kept them together was their consistent winning. And even that, finally, was not enough.

Foyt and Bignotti. Two fiercely proud men, each convinced that he was the best in the business at what he did. Neither particularly wanting, or accepting, the advice of the other. On good days, winning days, they would proclaim their respect and affection for one another.

"That Big George Notti," Foyt would say, "he's all right." And Bignotti, grinning shyly, would answer, "That's my driver."

But under the surface, tension always threatened to boil

over, and often did. Bignotti was the target of the fistful of sockets thrown by Foyt. When something about the team or a car bothered Foyt, Bignotti heard about it in no uncertain terms.

In the middle of the 1962 season, Foyt picked up his gear in Bignotti's garage, walked out, and joined car owner Lindsay Hopkins and mechanic Jack Beckley.

As a team, in 1960 and 1961, Foyt and Bignotti had won two national titles and the Indianapolis 500. Apart, neither was able to win. So before the season ended, they patched up their differences and got back together.

The pair came on strong again in 1963, winning the national title. And in 1964, with Bignotti still turning the wrenches, Foyt not only won at Indianapolis for the second time, but went on to an unprecedented fourth national championship. He won 10 of 13 races that year, a record unmatched in championship car racing.

In the midst of that winning streak, Foyt tried to explain his relationship with Bignotti. "George and I holler a lot at each other, but that's just our nature," he said. "We both want to win so badly that sometimes we just get to screaming. It really doesn't mean anything, though."

A year later, however, Foyt was suffering through one of his worst seasons. Before it was over, he and Bignotti had split again, this time for good.

The two fell to arguing in their garage at Indianapolis, summer headquarters for many racing teams. This time it was Bignotti who walked out, muttering that Foyt would never grow up. "I've had it this time," Bignotti said. "This is it." And it was, for the pair never got together again.

But Bignotti is by no means the only one who has been the target of Foyt's anger.

In 1962, after winning a 100-mile race in Milwaukee, Foyt figured that his prize money was short by $500. He threatened to punch out veteran promoter Tom Marchese because of it. Track personnel had to separate the two. If they had actually come to blows, it would have been disastrous for Marchese. Foyt, then 27, was a well-muscled six-footer. Marchese, well into his 60s, was a paunchy little fellow of five-five.

Foyt claimed that as defending national champion, he was owed the $500 in appearance money. Marchese tried to explain that the contracts for the race allowed appearance money only for that year's Indianapolis winner, in that case Rodger Ward.

Foyt cooled off overnight and the next day made a public apology, claiming that the whole thing had been a misunderstanding. Even so, he drew a $1,000 fine and a severe reprimand from USAC.

He came out better in his next big hassle, a year later. Following a sprint car race at Williams Grove, Pennsylvania, Foyt stormed into the pit occupied by Johnny White, a hot young driver from Detroit. Foyt charged that White had cut him off several times during the race.

According to a report filed with USAC by Eastern Zone Supervisor Tommy Nicholson, Foyt punctuated his complaint by slugging White, who still was buckled into his car. USAC put Foyt on indefinite suspension, but lifted it two days later because of conflicting reports on the incident. Foyt eventually was cleared of the charges.

Foyt has a few good friends among drivers, but he is respected more than he is liked. One reason may be that he has played some shrewd tricks on his rivals.

Foyt rather likes to be known as something of a sharpie. "If they're worrying about what I'm doing," he says, "then they aren't paying as much attention to their own business. That gives me an edge."

He said he once had his crew run a piece of tubing under one side of the car. The tube was a fake. But it served Foyt's purpose. Everybody on pit row got excited, wondering what new mechanical wrinkle he had come up with.

Another time, the exhaust from the engine in Foyt's car had a strange smell. That set everyone to guessing what new fuel additive Foyt had found.

"We just put a few drops of shoe polish in the tank," he said. "Had 'em all shook up."

Newspaper reporters and Foyt generally are not easy companions. Foyt thinks that his squabbles and blowups often are not reported fairly. And reporters figure that Foyt is not always exactly telling them the truth.

In 1966, Foyt crashed at Milwaukee and suffered burns that kept him out of racing for a few weeks. He still was not fully recovered when he ran next, in a 300-mile championship event at Atlanta. He was asked about the accident by an Atlanta reporter. The reporter wrote that Foyt had nothing but bad to say about the Milwaukee track and its operators.

"That Milwaukee is a Mickey Mouse operation," Foyt was quoted as saying. "One fireman just stood there when I was on fire. Why, I guess he'd have let me burn to death."

Later that season Foyt returned to Milwaukee for the annual Tony Bettenhausen 200-mile race at the Wisconsin State Fair. He denied the quotes attributed to him in Atlanta.

"I never knocked Milwaukee," he said. "In fact, I was telling them what good treatment I'd got here. The emergency crews have been good here.

"Besides, I don't know why they're talking in Atlanta. They're always bragging about their operation down there, but I don't think it's so hot."

Foyt likes to use the newspapers, though, when he wants to criticize USAC. Which is often. He frequently complains that USAC picks on him. But he's locked horns with the organization on other issues, too. He criticized the lightweight, rear-engine cars that replaced the traditional Indy roadster in the mid-1960s. And he was the leading opponent of the turbine-powered car when Andy Granatelli made turbine power practical for racing in 1967.

If Foyt seems a disagreeable sort, it's because he is. But not always. There is another side to him, a smooth side, that outsiders seldom see.

Drivers who have had words with Foyt sometimes are surprised by apologies. If a newspaper reporter is willing to wait long enough, Foyt usually will talk and answer questions. And in the right circumstances, he can be gracious, knowledgeable, and helpful.

He may be rough and forceful, but he is not necessarily unkind.

"What a lot of people don't understand is that his getting angry is his way of getting your attention," says Howard Gilbert, one of his crewmen. "He's really not so rough. In fact, I think it's sort of a coverup. He's the softest guy. Just can't say no to people.

"You know, he wrote off an awful lot of parts and stuff to other drivers last year. When they need something, they come around because they know he's too good-hearted to turn them down."

Foyt also campaigns loudly for greater safety precautions in racing. He accepts the dangers that go with racing. "I just figure if I die, I'll die doing something I want to do," he says. "How many people can do that?

"But racing doesn't have to be suicidal. I've been burned four times, and let me tell you, it's not any fun. I don't want to be burned again. And I don't like to see my friends get hurt, either."

On some occasions, Foyt has agreed to race just to give a hard-pressed promoter a genuine drawing card.

He is not one-dimensional. He is a man of many moods, many feelings. But if there's an argument at the racetrack, look for Foyt somewhere in the middle of it.

Peaks and Valleys

The amazing thing about A. J. Foyt is not that he has won so many races. That's impressive. But not amazing.

The amazing thing is that he has won so many races over so long a period of time.

Auto racing is a very streaky sport. A hot driver in a hot car will win often — but usually just for a short period of time. Then, in a season or two, often less, somebody else will have the hot setup. And *he* will be the driver to beat.

Since Foyt became a serious contender in the late 1950s, there have been lots of hot drivers in hot cars. Rodger Ward, Parnelli Jones, Scotsman Jim Clark, Mario Andretti, Bobby Unser, Al Unser, Joe Leonard, and Mark Donohue all became famous in Foyt's time. They all enjoyed hot streaks, and made the most of them.

Foyt, too, has at times been the hot driver in the hot car. The difference is, he has had so many more hot streaks. Since 1960, when Foyt won his first national title, there have been only three seasons in which he failed to score a championship car victory.

That does not mean that once Foyt reached the top, all he had to do was enjoy it. Far from it. He has been down, too. And, from time to time, there have been those who figured his career was all but over.

In the four seasons between 1969 and the start of 1973, for instance, Foyt won only two national championship races. He was winning occasionally in stock cars, but seldom in Indy cars. He had taken over development and distribution of the Ford racing engine, but the Offenhauser engine was making a big comeback. Foyt was suffering.

But in 1973, he came back with two victories. Then he scored two more in 1974. And in 1975, he showed that neither he nor the Ford engine — by then renamed the Foyt engine — was through. He started the new season with an impressive victory in the California 500 at Ontario, and won six of his first eight races, clinching his sixth national championship.

It is his ability to come back from difficult, frustrating periods that sets Foyt apart from so many of the other good drivers.

Among his other qualities, Foyt has a flair for the dramatic. Perhaps that, as much as anything, explains the ups and downs of his career. He may be up, or he may be down. But very seldom is he ordinary. When he is up, he tends to be way up. And when he is down, he tends to be way down.

And sometimes, strange as it may seem, he is both at the same time.

Take his 1964 season. It was, by any yardstick, the greatest season any championship car driver has ever had. Foyt won the first seven races on USAC's championship trail, among them the Indianapolis 500 for the second time. He finished the season with 10 victories in 13 races.

When he finally lost, in the eighth race of the season, he really lost. And it deserves some explanation.

In 1963, there was a great revolution in championship car racing. For years, the heavy roadster, with its reliable four-cylinder Offenhauser engine mounted in front of the driver, had been the conventional style car. But in Europe, on the Grand Prix circuit for Formula One cars, there had been a change.

In an effort to get more speed from limited engines, Formula One designers had done away with the heavy frame design and moved the engines behind the drivers. The Ford V-8 was rapidly becoming the dominant powerplant. The most successful of the new breed Formula One designers was Colin Chapman of England. His cars bore the name Lotus.

Most American drivers laughed at the rear-engine lightweights. They called them "funny cars." They laughed until Jim Clark and Dan Gurney drove Chapman's cars to second and seventh place finishes in the 500. Then, suddenly, the rear-engine lightweights were cars to be respected and feared. It became pretty obvious that car owners would soon have to junk their thousands of dollars' worth of equipment and change over to the new-style car and the new Ford engine.

It became even more obvious later that season, when Jim Clark, in a Lotus-Ford, ran away from the field in the Tony Bettenhausen 200 at Milwaukee. His convincing victory was the first for the rear-engine lightweights in America.

Of course, some drivers continued to scoff at the new cars, and many thought they were too light to be safe. Foyt was one of those drivers.

29

"Truthfully, I don't like the funny cars," he said. "I don't think they are proven yet and I don't feel they are completely safe. They are fast cars, and they are the coming thing. But if we don't get them fixed so I'll feel completely safe, I just won't drive one of them." But he did. And eventually, so did everybody else. But that's getting ahead of the story.

Early in the 1964 season, Foyt still was driving his roadster. The Lotus-Fords didn't do well at Indianapolis, but mostly because of poor tires, an English brand designed for road racing. Foyt outlasted the new-style cars and won the race.

In August, Chapman put his Lotus-Fords on American-made tires and entered them in the Tony Bettenhausen 200-mile race at Milwaukee. Chapman wanted top drivers for his cars, but his regulars, Jim Clark and Dan Gurney, both were busy on the Formula One circuit. He finally talked Parnelli Jones into driving one of the cars. And then he talked Foyt into driving the other — the same Foyt who had won seven straight races in his roadster.

If Foyt had misgivings about the switch, he soon learned that those misgivings were justified.

Jones, taking to the new-style car as if he had been born in it, drove to an almost effortless victory.

And Foyt? Foyt's seven-race winning streak was nipped in the first minute of competition. He completed one lap and part of another. Then the car's transmission failed. He was the first driver out of the race. The man who had won all seven previous races that year finished dead last.

The rear-engine, lightweight design was here to stay, though, and Foyt, along with everyone else, had to accept it.

If 1964 was Foyt's finest season, 1965 was in many ways his worst. It got off to a terrible start at the Riverside, California, 500-mile stock car road race. The brakes in Foyt's car failed, and he pitched over a steep embankment. He suffered a broken back, among other less serious injuries.

By the end of March, Foyt had recovered enough to drive again, but car failure took him out of championship events at Phoenix, Arizona, and Trenton, New Jersey. Then, while he was practicing at Indianapolis, a structural weakness in Foyt's Lotus-Ford caused him to crash again. He escaped serious injury, but the little faith he had in his car was dwindling. His relations with George Bignotti were going downhill, too.

Jim Clark dominated that year's 500. Foyt, for a time, seemed the only driver who might possibly catch the flying Scotsman, but a broken gearbox took him out of the running early.

Foyt was pretty depressed. "It just seems like this year I can't do anything right," he said. "I started out the year by almost getting killed at Riverside. I sat in the front row of every race I started, but couldn't finish. Now this.

"I'm pretty disappointed. I think I just might quit racing. I really want to think it over for a couple of days."

Of course, he didn't quit. He showed up about a week later for the Rex Mays 100-miler in Milwaukee, right on schedule and as feisty as ever. "I never said I was going to quit," he said. "I wasn't even considering it."

Foyt eventually pulled out of his tailspin and finished with five victories on the championship trail. And in that same season, he drove one of his most memorable races. Surprisingly, it was one he didn't win.

It was August, state fair time in Wisconsin and Illinois. State fair time in those states means more than produce and livestock. It also means racing. Drivers shuttle back and forth from Milwaukee to Springfield for a series of stock and championship car events.

On a Saturday afternoon, Foyt drove his dirt track champion-

ship car to victory on the one-mile dirt track at Springfield. Then he left for Milwaukee and the Sunday afternoon Bettenhausen 200 on the asphalt track there. His Lotus-Ford, the car he used on paved tracks, was supposed to be there when he arrived. But it never showed up. Foyt was left with nothing to drive but his old-fashioned dirt track car. Surely he wouldn't try that, would he?

Oh, wouldn't he! He not only tried — he made it work. After qualifying was over, who was on the pole, who was fastest? It was Foyt, sitting bolt upright in the antique dirt tracker, looking down upon the other guys reclining in their hot new stuff.

That wasn't the end of it, either. Once the race got started, it was obvious that some other cars were faster. They weren't necessarily stronger, though. When it was over, Gordon Johncock had won. But Foyt had led twice, and finished second.

He probably has not been happier about a second-place finish before or since. He complained about his back hurting and said, "Man, was that only 200 miles? I must have drove at least a thousand." But his eyes were shining and he was a happy, happy driver. "Man, if I'd won this race, everybody'd be going back to front Offies next year," he chortled.

There have been other good times — and bad — for Foyt. In 1966, his first full season without Bignotti, he failed to win a championship race. And he lost another mechanic.

Foyt had picked up Johnny Pouelsen, formerly with Parnelli Jones, when Bignotti left. They were working on Foyt's cars late one August afternoon at Indianapolis. Foyt decided that they should keep working until one balky car was set right. Pouelsen agreed, but said he wanted to get something to eat first.

"I said we're going to stay until we get it fixed," Foyt said. He added that if Pouelsen left, he could consider himself fired. Pouelsen walked out, returned the next day to pick up

33

his equipment, then sold it all. He had had enough of Foyt, enough of racing.

Foyt stayed with it, though, and was back on top the next season. He won at Indianapolis, for the third time, and at LeMans. He won another national championship in 1967, and USAC's stock car title in 1968. Always, it seemed, he was able to come back.

"I look at it this way," he once said. "You can't relax or you fall behind. Mother told me years ago that when you get to the top, there is only one way to go—down. But I'm still on top."

The Checkered Flag

A. J. Foyt always has been known as a hard-charging driver. His idea of fun on the track is to get out in front as fast as he can and stay there—right through the checkered flag.

At times, though, even the hardest-charging drivers have to play the waiting game. It is very much a part of racing. When other cars are faster, there is little a driver can do about it on race day. If he still wants to win the race, the best thing he can do is stay as close as he can to the faster cars. He tries very hard not to make mistakes. And he waits.

He waits for the faster cars to have problems. He waits for the drivers in the faster cars to make mistakes.

Sometimes, he spends the whole race waiting while somebody else runs off with the victory. But very often, the things he is waiting for do happen. Very often, the patient driver is first to get the checkered flag.

Surprisingly, considering his reputation, Foyt has scored many of his victories by waiting. In fact, that's how he won his three victories in the Indianapolis 500. There is an old racetrack expression that says, "To finish first, first you must finish." Foyt understands that very well.

Foyt's first Indianapolis victory, in 1961, was one of the most unusual he has scored. At times it appeared that neither he nor Eddie Sachs, the man he eventually beat, would be able to finish, much less win.

It was a very competitive race. Seven drivers led it, and the lead changed hands 20 times. As the race wore on, most of the top drivers fell out of the running or back into the pack. With 40 laps (100 miles) left, the race was between Foyt and Sachs. Each had made his third, and supposedly final, pit stop. Each was ready to race the other to the checker.

Foyt charged ahead, then Sachs caught and passed him. Then it was Foyt again, moving ahead and opening a 10-second lead. It appeared that the race would be his.

But suddenly Foyt began signaling his crew that he was running low on fuel. With 16 laps left, he had to return to his pit. On his previous stop, the pressure fueling system had failed. Unknown to either Foyt or his crew, no fuel had gone into the car. Ten gallons of alcohol were quickly added on his emergency stop, but that took 15 seconds. By the time

Foyt got rolling and back up to racing speed, Sachs was 31 seconds ahead. There was no way Foyt could catch him before the end of the race. So he waited.

And soon, there was Sachs, signaling to his crew that something was wrong with his car. His right rear tire was wearing out. He tried to make it last, but he couldn't. The rubber wore thin, peeled away, and exposed a layer of canvas put there to warn drivers to go no farther on that tire. So, with just three laps left, Sachs had to come in.

A. J. went by as Sachs returned to the track. Foyt won the race by eight seconds.

Foyt's second Indianapolis victory, in 1964, was not nearly so difficult. In fact, it was almost easy, once he moved into the lead. But first, he had to wait.

The big threats that year were Jim Clark and Bobby Marshman in Lotus-Fords, Rodger Ward in a new rear-engine Watson-Ford, and Parnelli Jones and Foyt in their conventional Offenhauser-powered roadsters.

The race was barely underway when a fiery crash at the top of the homestretch stopped the action. Sachs and Dave MacDonald, a successful young road racer competing for the first time at Indianapolis, were burned to death.

Nearly two hours were needed to clear the track of the wreckage, but when the race was finally resumed, Marshman drove off to a big lead.

Marshman was running 30 seconds ahead of Jim Clark when suddenly he pulled off the track. A small piece of wreckage on the track had cut his car's oil line. The leak was bad enough to force Marshman out of the running.

Then Clark took over. His lead lasted only six laps, however. His English-made road racing tires were not up to the pounding and wear tires get at Indianapolis. The tires caused his car's suspension system to break down. Dan

37

Gurney, Clark's teammate, was called in for the same tire problems.

That left the race to Jones, Foyt, and Ward. And Jones was ready to take it. He moved ahead and held the lead for seven laps, then pulled in for a regularly scheduled pit stop. He never got out of the pit. His crew, eager to get him back on the track, accidentally spilled fuel on his car's hot engine. It caught fire just as Jones was rolling out of the pit, blowing the almost-invisible alcohol flames right toward him. He shut off the car's engine and jumped out, rolling on the concrete and beating at his burning coveralls. He escaped with minor burns, but his race was over.

That left Foyt and Ward. Foyt was ready. Ward wasn't. On the 55th lap of the 200-lap race, Foyt took the lead and held it the rest of the way.

In 1967, Foyt had to wait a long time before he could call the Indianapolis victory his. That was the year of the turbocar, owner Andy Granatelli's turbine-powered racer. The turbine engine made almost no noise and the car was quickly dubbed the Whooshmobile. Parnelli Jones, the driver, called it Silent Sam.

The car caused lots of bad feelings at the track, and Foyt was among its loudest critics. "The Indianapolis Motor Speedway has always been a proving ground for automobiles, not airplanes," Foyt said. The turbine engine in Jones' car was similar to jet engines used in planes and helicopters.

Just the same, the car was within the limits of the rules at the time, and Jones drove it brilliantly.

Jones, starting sixth, was in second place going into the first turn, and was leading going into the second. He had half a lap on the field after 18 laps, when rain stopped the race for the rest of the day. When it was resumed the next day, Jones gave the fans more of the same. He led, and led, and led, building up a 54-second advantage with only four laps left. Without a doubt, it was his race.

Without a doubt? Not quite.

On the 197th lap, the quick-change bearing broke in the car's gearbox, leaving the car with no gears and no power. Jones had done all of the leading, but he wasn't able to finish. Foyt won, threading his way through a four-car crash at the top of the straightaway on the last lap.

"I had a funny feeling I might win this race," Foyt said. "We were pretty well prepared and we hadn't had any trouble all month (in practice). I didn't try to run with Parnelli in the turbine, though. There's just no way to run with a turbine. I figured the turbine would run maybe 100 laps. When Parnelli finished 100 laps, why, I just figured he was home free. All I wanted to do then was stay on the same lap with him, so in case something did happen, I'd be right up there."

Only 12 days later, Foyt showed his style to the folks on the other side of the Atlantic. He and Dan Gurney got together to drive a Ford Mark IV to victory in the LeMans 24-hour

endurance race for sports cars. The LeMans classic is regarded in Europe, and much of the rest of the world, as the biggest race anywhere.

The Ferrari team of Italy was the big threat to the American Ford team, but Gurney and Foyt turned the race into no contest. They smashed one record after another, leading all the way as they became the first American team ever to win the race in an American-built car. They completed 388 laps over the 8.3-mile road course, for 3,220.4 miles at an average speed of 135.482 miles per hour. There was no waiting by Foyt in this one.

"It was easy," he said. "I feel good coming over here and stealing this race from the sports car drivers." He admitted, though, that he still liked Indianapolis better. When someone asked why, he replied, "The money." European races may be great for glory, but they don't pay as much as American races.

Victory in NASCAR's big race, the Daytona 500, eluded Foyt for years. He had won other major stock car races, but the biggest of them all had escaped him. He nailed that down in February of 1972.

Driving a Mercury for the Wood Brothers team of Stuart, Virginia, he raced to an overwhelming triumph. He led for 167 of the 200 laps, and finished a full lap ahead of second place Charlie Glotzbach's Chevrolet. Only two other drivers, Richard Petty and Bobby Allison, led the race, and then only briefly.

"I've won at Indy three times and I've won at LeMans," Foyt said. "I had wanted to win the Daytona 500 because this is the greatest stock car race in the world."

It was back to waiting, though, for Foyt in the 1973 Pocono 500 for championship cars.

And once again, it appeared that waiting wouldn't be quite good enough. Roger McCluskey held off a challenge by Foyt for nearly 100 miles. McCluskey went into the last lap with half a lap lead on Foyt. But he never finished that last lap. His car ran out of fuel, and Foyt came around to take the checkered flag first.

Foyt chuckled. "I have said many times that it's the last lap that counts," he said.

The California 500 at Ontario in 1975 was Foyt's to do with as he pleased. He pleased to win. So he did, throttling the field. He led for all but 12 of the 200 laps over the 2.5-mile track, an almost identical twin to the Indianapolis Speedway, and finished nearly a lap ahead of Bobby Unser.

Since the Ontario race was the first of the 1975 season, Foyt was in a position to become the first driver ever to win USAC's Triple Crown. The Triple Crown series is made up of the 500-mile races at Ontario, Indianapolis, and Mt. Pocono, Pennsylvania.

He was the favorite going into the Indianapolis 500, but

finished third. An accident involving Tom Sneva left debris on the track, and Foyt was forced to make an unplanned pit stop to change cut tires. Before he could catch up to the leading Bobby Unser, rain stopped the race.

But he came back strong in the Pocono 500, another rain-shortened race, winning it for the second time in three years. He said he won because of a lesson he had learned just weeks earlier at Indianapolis.

He was running low on fuel during the Pocono race, but he skipped a planned pit stop. He stretched a lead of several car lengths to 300 yards over Wally Dallenbach before heavy rain fell with 30 laps left.

"I hung back at Indianapolis, waiting to make my move, and what happens? The rain washes out the last 25 laps and I'm stuck in third," he said. "I kept my eyes on the sky when I could. I could see the rain clouds coming in there at the end, so I turned up the power all the way to go for broke."

He missed the Triple Crown, settling for two-thirds of it. But winning two of three 500-mile races still rates as a job well done, even for so fussy a man as Foyt.

The Financial Foyt

"I run to win," Foyt has said. "I don't care if I win $100,000 or $1,000, I just want to win."

There have been times when Foyt has gone out of his way to prove that.

There was the time at Terre Haute, Indiana, for instance. Foyt was scheduled to drive a sprint car program there. But it rained hard almost until race time. The dirt track was so muddy that none of the drivers wanted to race. First prize in the feature race that day was only $600. It was not a risk worth taking.

But the promoter had a crowd on hand. He wanted to put on a race. He asked Foyt to qualify, hoping that Foyt would set an example for the others. Foyt agreed. He went out onto the muddy track, slid around as best he could, and took a slow qualifying time.

As he was finishing, the sun finally broke through. The other drivers agreed to wait until the track was dry, then they qualified. Naturally, with the track in better condition, many of them qualified faster than Foyt had. The field for the feature was made up of 24 cars. Foyt's car was 25th fastest. He was out of the race.

But Foyt had an idea. He went to the driver of the 24th car and offered him $100 for the use of the car in the feature. The

43

deal was accepted. Foyt started the race in last place.

He didn't stay there long. He passed seven cars on the first lap, and before long had passed everyone else. He gave that car the ride of its life, and coasted to a thumping victory. And he did coast. The car ran out of fuel on the last lap, but Foyt was so far ahead by then that he was able to finish on momentum and still win.

He has frequently left the Indianapolis Speedway during the practice month of May to race another type of car somewhere else. In 1974, in fact, he tuned up for the Indy 500 by running, and winning, a sprint car program on the dirt at the Indiana State Fairgrounds in Indianapolis. That was two nights before the big show at the Speedway.

But there is no point in trying to separate money from racing. It is there, a fact of life. Money and racing are tied up in one giant, complicated knot. And there is no point, either, in trying to keep Foyt and money on separate levels.

Through racing, and because of it, he has become a very rich man.

He was auto racing's first millionaire. He now is a millionaire several times over, and the longer he stays with it, the wealthier he becomes.

At the start, Foyt was no better than any other young driver working his way up. He drove for a percentage of his car's winnings, usually about 40%. The rest went to the car owner and crew.

When it became obvious that Foyt was a genuine star, he became worth more. His share of the winnings went up to 50%. Later still, he was able to command that 50%, plus a yearly salary from his car owners. And as his fame grew, sponsors wanted to tie up with him. Not with his car or his car owner, but with him. They paid him to promote their products.

Eventually, Foyt reached the point where he could go it

alone, without a car owner. He formed his own team, hired his own designer, built his own cars, and kept greater shares of his winnings.

He made outside investments, too. There were stock deals and real estate. Texas oil wells. A car dealership in Houston. He bought a chicken farm, then a cattle ranch. Goodyear paid him to test and run his cars on its tires. Ford paid him to run their cars and engines. Eventually, Ford turned its championship car-racing engine program over to him.

Foyt's business deals have been successful. They probably have brought him more money than his racing. As one of his sponsors once said, "He may have dropped out of high school, but he sure knows how to read a contract."

At his cattle ranch, Foyt also runs a string of quarter horses, that tough little western strain of horse bred to cover a quarter of a mile very quickly.

Foyt takes a great deal of interest in his horses. Early in the 1975 season, he qualified for the annual Rex Mays 150-mile race in Milwaukee. On his first qualifying lap, his car hit a small hump in the track, became airborne and almost crashed. Foyt gathered up the car on the second lap, though, and ran it fast enough to win the pole. When he was done, what did he want to talk about? Winning the pole for the next day's race? His near miss on that first qualifying lap?

Not at all. Foyt walked down pit row to see Wally Dallenbach, another driver who recently had bought a ranch in Colorado. "You know," Foyt said, "I sure hope my horse has a good day tomorrow. He's running for a whole pile of money."

Still, above everything else for Foyt, there is racing.

"I don't want to quit," he says. "Racing is my life. When I quit, it will be like ending my life."

But nobody, not even Foyt, can go on racing forever. Eventually he will have to step out of the cockpit for the last

time and walk away from the speed, the winning, the cheers of the crowds. Then his many business ventures will become even more important to him. He is not the sort of man who will sit around, waiting for something to happen.

His place in auto racing history is assured, but Foyt claims not to care much about that. "I don't care how they remember me," he said. "If they want to remember me, fine. If not, I don't care.

"If they want to remember me as a great race driver, fine. If they want to remember me as a heel, that's fine, too. All I know is that I've never been a put-on, or a fake."

Design   **Interface Design Group Inc.**